Animals
Through the Year

Fang

Published by Raintree Steck-Vaughn Publishers, an imprint of Steck-Vaughn Company

Library of Congress Cataloging-in-Publication Data

Potter, Tessa.
Fang, the story of a fox in winter / story by Tessa Potter; illustrations by Ken Lilly.
p.   cm. — (Animals through the year)
Summary: A young fox experiences his first winter as he looks for food, interacts with other animals in the Great Woods, and finds a safe place to sleep.
ISBN 0-8172-4622-3
1. Red fox — Juvenile fiction.   [1. Red fox — Fiction.   2. Foxes — Fiction.]
I. Lilly, Kenneth, ill.   II. Title.   III. Series.
PZ10.3.P645Fan   1997
[Fic] — dc21   96-38990
                                                                                          CIP   AC

With thanks to Bernard Thornton Artists

The author would like to thank Dr. Gerald Legg of the
Booth Museum of Natural History, Brighton, for his help and advice.

Color separated in Switzerland by Photolitho AG, Offsetreproduktionen, Gossau, Zurich.

Printed and bound in the United States.

1 2 3 4 5 6 7 8 9 0 IP 00 99 98 97 96

Fang

Animals
Through the Year

The Story of a Fox in Winter

Story by Tessa Potter
Illustrations by Ken Lilly

RSVP

RAINTREE STECK-VAUGHN
P U B L I S H E R S
The Steck-Vaughn Company

Austin, Texas

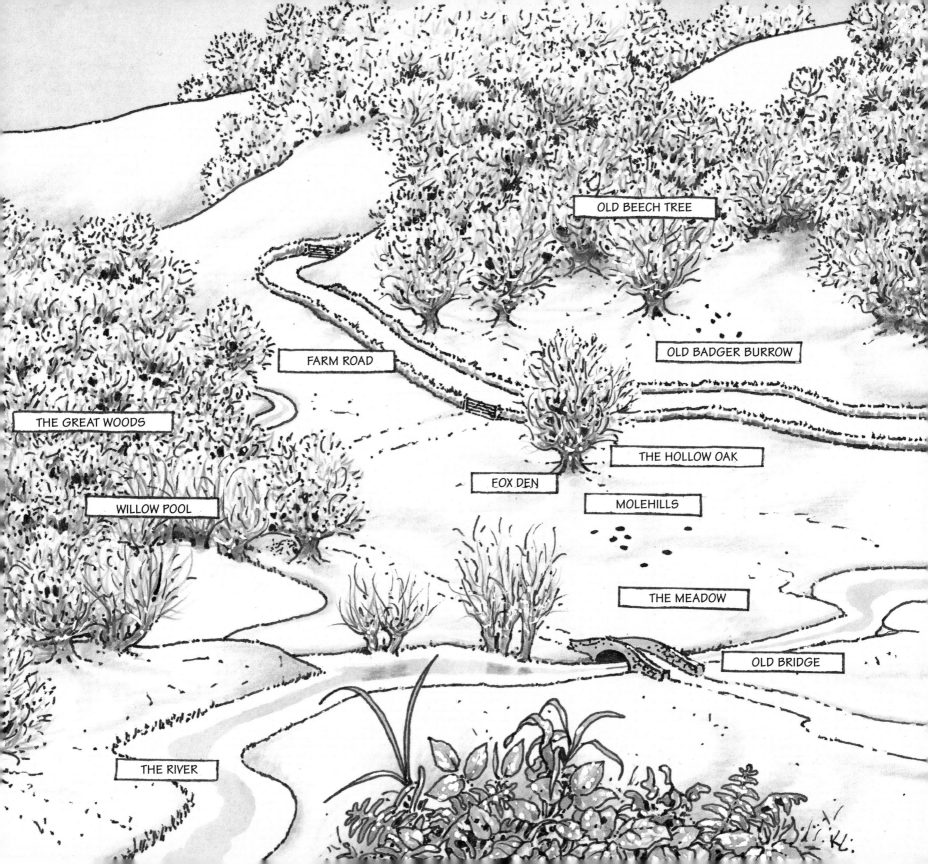

OLD BEECH TREE

OLD BADGER BURROW

FARM ROAD

THE GREAT WOODS

THE HOLLOW OAK

FOX DEN

WILLOW POOL

MOLEHILLS

THE MEADOW

OLD BRIDGE

THE RIVER

For five days a white frost had gripped the woods, freezing
the ground and turning the bare twigs and branches silver.
Only the otters on Kingfisher Bank enjoyed the cold; throwing
themselves time after time down the slippery, icy banks.
In the Great Woods a mole was digging under one
of her tunnels, looking for worms where the
earth was not so cold. And under a hollow tree,
a young fox was taking shelter from the cold.
It was Fang, and this was his first winter.

A sudden scream in the still night made Fang stir in his sleep. He buried his nose deeper into his bushy tail. It was a vixen, a female fox, calling her mate from her den above the Sheep Pasture. Her call was answered by an old dog fox, who crossed the river and began to make his way through the Great Woods. He trotted along the same trails Fang had used since the autumn, stopping now and then to leave his mark.

Shortly before dawn, the first snow began to fall. By early morning a thick blanket covered the ground. Fang uncurled and stretched. He was hungry. As he crept outside, he noticed a strong smell. He saw a fresh yellow stain near the entrance to his den and knew immediately that another fox had left his mark and was moving through his territory. Fang quickly made a new mark of his own and then set off uneasily through the wood toward Willow Pool.

The birds were cold and hungry. Fang was hoping he could catch one easily. As he went near the pool, he heard a noise from the far side. He saw a young swan struggling in the reeds, its legs caught in the ice. Fang crept out onto the frozen pond and moved slowly toward the trapped bird.

Suddenly, a huge male swan
flew at him, hissing furiously.
Fang turned and ran, his
feet skidding on the ice.

15

As Fang ran away through the woods, he again smelled the scent of the other fox. He hurried on, wanting only to find food. Perhaps there would be rabbits on Burrow Hill. But the hill was deserted. Only the crows flew overhead. As he crept along Thornbush Hedge, Fang heard a faint scratching sound. He stood very still. A field vole was tunneling under the snow. This time he knew he would be lucky.

It was at that moment that Fang saw him. The old dog fox had crept up the far side of the bank and slipped through a gap in the hedge. Fang growled and stood his ground. But as the large male fox moved toward him with a snarling scream, Fang knew he didn't stand a chance. He cowered low on the ground. He felt snarling jaws close to his face. This was no play fight. This fox meant to hurt him.

Fang was very frightened.
He began to run, away from the
Great Woods. He ran toward
Farm Road. A car was going
too fast down the icy road.

Fang saw nothing. He heard a
screech of brakes and a thud as he
was flung to the edge of the road.

Fang was stunned and badly bruised. For a while he lay very still, then he dragged himself up and limped away into the trees. His leg hurt. He desperately wanted food and a safe shelter. At last, he found an old log and scraped away the decaying wood. There were slugs and beetle larvae. He snapped them up quickly and began to feel a little better.

It was late afternoon when Fang reached an empty badger burrow. As he crawled inside, a family of wood mice scattered. He was too tired now to think of food. He licked his throbbing leg to ease the pain. He needed to sleep. He felt safe here. Perhaps this would be his new home.

Look back at the story.
Can you find...

A young **swan**.
The young swan's legs
are caught in the ice.

A **rabbit** out looking for food.

A **snowdrop**.

A **deceiver fungus**.

A **queen bumblebee**. Only the
queen bumblebee will survive
the winter. She will lay
her eggs in the spring.

A **pygmy shrew** that has
not survived the winter. It
needed to find food every two
or three hours to stay alive.

A **gray squirrel** climbing a
silver birch tree.

A **deer mouse**.

A **blackbird**.

A **great gray slug** hiding in a log.

Trailing wolfsbane.

A **long-eared bat** hibernating in a hollow tree.

Cattails.

A **toad** hibernating under a log.

A **ladybug** sheltering for the winter. Ladybugs cluster together and have a special smell that keeps predators away.

A **stag beetle pupa** hidden in a rotting log. The stag beetle will hatch in the spring.

A **mole** digging her tunnel.

An **orange sulphur butterfly** hibernating among some ivy leaves. With its wings closed, it looks just like a leaf and is safe from hungry birds.

An **oyster fungus**.

An **otter** playing in the snow.

A **rose hip**.

A **deer** hiding in the wood. It is hard to spot among the trees, but you may find its droppings close by.

A **mouse's** nest in the brambles.

THINGS TO DO

MAKING A BIRD FEEDING AREA
Here are some ways to attract
birds to your garden.

BIRD FEEDERS
Put some bird food in a
milk carton and hang from
a tree or clothesline.

HANGING BIRD FOOD
Thread a string through an old yogurt container and tie a matchstick on the
end. Mix some bird food with some melted fat and spoon it into the pot.
When the mixture is hard, pull it out and hang it outside.

Look for these birds in your garden:

WATCHING BIRDS
To watch the birds close up
without disturbing them,
you can make a simple
blind by taping a sheet of
paper over a window that
looks out onto your garden.
Make holes for your eyes.

| house finch | plain titmouse | Carolina chicadee | cardinal | red-winged blackbird | hermit thrush | starling | house sparrow | robin |

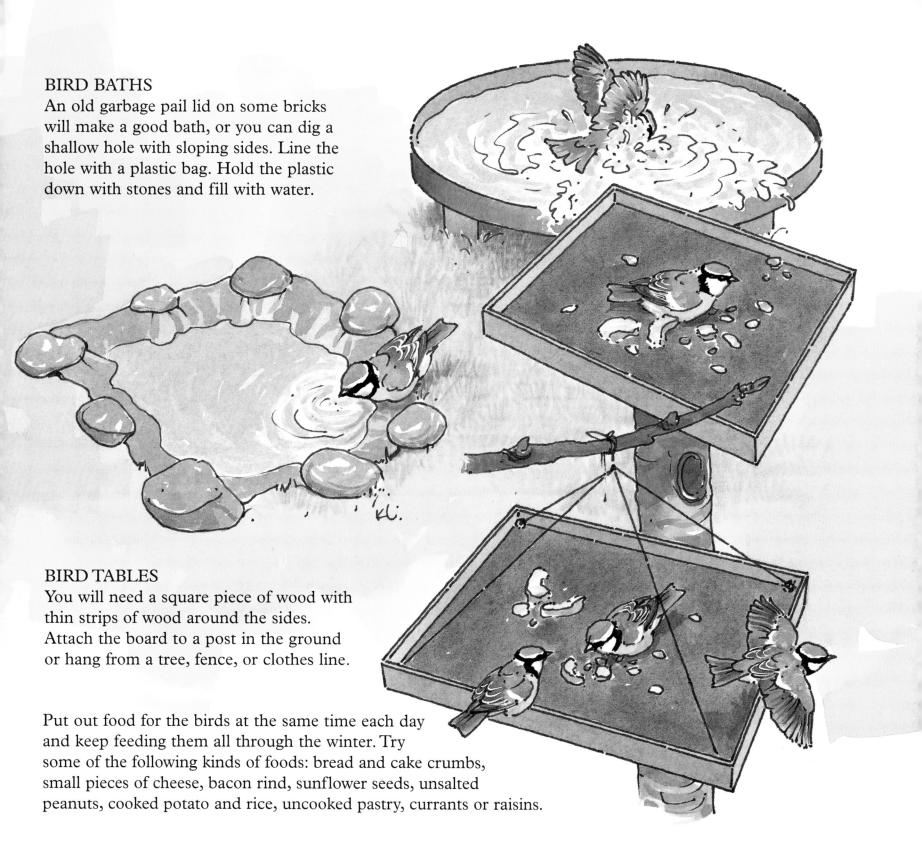

BIRD BATHS

An old garbage pail lid on some bricks will make a good bath, or you can dig a shallow hole with sloping sides. Line the hole with a plastic bag. Hold the plastic down with stones and fill with water.

BIRD TABLES

You will need a square piece of wood with thin strips of wood around the sides. Attach the board to a post in the ground or hang from a tree, fence, or clothes line.

Put out food for the birds at the same time each day and keep feeding them all through the winter. Try some of the following kinds of foods: bread and cake crumbs, small pieces of cheese, bacon rind, sunflower seeds, unsalted peanuts, cooked potato and rice, uncooked pastry, currants or raisins.

MORE ABOUT FOXES

Books

Burton, Jane. *Trill, the Fox Cub*. Gareth Stevens, 1989

Butterworth, Christine and Gailey, Donna. *Foxes*. Raintree, Steck-Vaughn, 1990

Lepthien, Emilie U. and Kalbacken, Joan. *Foxes*. Childrens, 1993

Ling, Mary. *Amazing Wolves, Dogs, and Foxes*. Knopf, 1991

Markert, Jenny. *Arctic Foxes*. Childs World, 1991

Mason, Cherie. *Wild Fox: A True Story*. Down East, 1995

Wallace, Karen. *Red Fox*. Candlewick, 1994

Videos

Exploring the World of Mammals. (30 min.) Busch Entertainment, Batavia, Ohio: Video Treasures, 1992

Life on Earth. Episode 10. (58 min.) BBC/Warner Brothers. Films, Inc. distributor. Naturalist David Attenborough on mammals, 1988

See How They Grow. (30 min.) Includes wild animals, rabbits, foxes. Dorling Kindersley. Sony Kids' Video, 1995

First published in 1996 by Andersen Press